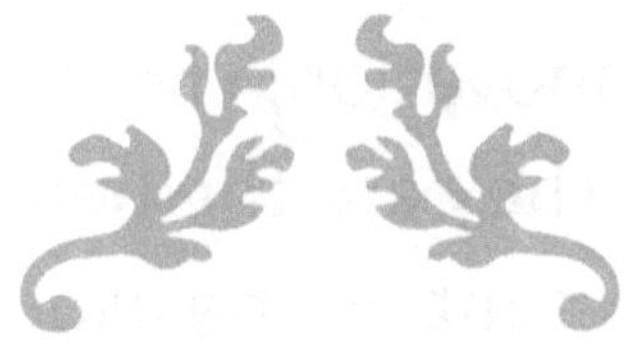

SMALL BUSINESS MASTERY

TAX PLANNING AND SCALING STRATEGIES

2023

DOBBS MEDIA

Introduction: Small Business Mastery

In the vast and ever-evolving landscape of the global economy, small businesses stand as the vibrant engines that fuel innovation, create jobs, and drive economic growth. They are the heart and soul of communities, representing the aspirations and hard work of countless individuals who dare to dream, create, and take risks. Welcome to "Small Business Mastery: Tax Planning and Scaling Strategies," where we embark on a journey to explore the critical elements that define and empower the world of small business management.

The Vital Role of Small Businesses

Small businesses have long been the lifeblood of economies around the world. They represent a diverse tapestry of entrepreneurial dreams, from corner stores and family-run restaurants to tech startups and creative agencies. Despite their size, small businesses collectively make an outsized impact, contributing significantly to job creation, economic stability, and local development.

Consider this: Small businesses account for a significant portion of job opportunities globally, offering employment to millions of people. These ventures provide opportunities for individuals to transform their skills, talents, and passions into sustainable livelihoods. They infuse life into communities, fostering a sense of connection and shared purpose that extends far beyond the confines of their storefronts or virtual platforms.

In addition to job creation, small businesses foster innovation and competition. They challenge established norms and drive advancements in products, services, and customer experiences. Small businesses are agile and adaptable, capable of responding swiftly to market shifts and consumer demands. They offer a diverse array of choices to consumers, enriching the marketplace and ensuring that the customer's voice remains influential.

However, small businesses face their own unique set of challenges, which often distinguish them from their larger counterparts. Limited resources, financial constraints, and the need to wear multiple hats can create formidable obstacles. The path to success can be winding and fraught with uncertainty, making it essential for small business owners to possess a deep understanding of various aspects of entrepreneurship.

Navigating the Challenges of Small Business Management

The road to small business success is anything but linear. Small business owners must grapple with a multitude of responsibilities, from product development and marketing to financial management and customer service. They must strike a delicate balance between innovation and stability, continually adapting to changing market conditions while upholding the values that define their brand.

One of the most daunting challenges small business owners face is the management of limited resources. Capital is often scarce, requiring careful allocation to ensure sustainable growth. Time, too, is a precious commodity, as entrepreneurs must maximize their productivity while minimizing inefficiencies.

Furthermore, small businesses operate within a complex web of regulations and legal requirements.

Understanding tax laws, employment regulations, and industry-specific rules is crucial to maintaining compliance and avoiding costly legal complications.

Navigating these challenges necessitates a combination of knowledge, strategy, and resilience. Small business owners must continually educate themselves, seek mentorship, and cultivate a growth mindset to overcome obstacles and seize opportunities.

The Power of Tax Planning and Scaling

In the pages of this book, we will delve deep into two critical pillars of small business success: tax planning and scaling. These are not mere buzzwords but strategic imperatives that can elevate your business from surviving to thriving.

Tax planning is an art that can significantly impact your business's bottom line. It involves understanding the tax code, optimizing deductions, and leveraging incentives to minimize your tax liability legally. Effective tax planning frees up capital that can be reinvested in your business or used to bolster your financial security.

Scaling, on the other hand, is about strategically expanding your business operations to reach new heights. It's a journey that involves calculated risks, sustainable growth strategies, and a keen understanding of market dynamics. Scaling is not a one-size-fits-all endeavor; it requires a tailored approach that aligns with your business's unique goals and circumstances.

Together, tax planning and scaling form a powerful synergy. By mastering both, you can not only navigate the complex terrain of small business management but also position your enterprise for long-term success and prosperity. In the chapters that follow, we will equip you with the knowledge, tools, and insights needed to master these critical aspects of entrepreneurship.

As you embark on this journey, remember that the challenges you face are opportunities in disguise, and your small business has the potential to make an indelible mark on your life, your community, and the world. Small business ownership is a testament to your courage, resilience, and determination. "Small Business Mastery: Tax Planning and Scaling

Strategies" is your trusted guide on this exciting adventure. Let's begin.

Chapter 1: The Foundation of Small Business Success

In the world of small business management, laying a strong foundation is the first step towards building a successful enterprise. This chapter explores the essential elements that form the bedrock of your business's success.

Defining Your Business Purpose and Vision

Every successful small business begins with a clear and compelling purpose. Your business purpose is the "why" behind what you do, the driving force that fuels your passion and motivates you to overcome challenges. It defines the impact you want to make on the world and the values that guide your decisions.

Take the time to reflect on your business purpose. What problem does your business solve, or what need does it fulfill? What values and principles will guide your actions as an entrepreneur? Articulating your purpose not only inspires you but also communicates your brand's identity to customers, employees, and stakeholders.

A closely aligned component of your business purpose is your vision. Your vision is your long-term goal—a vivid picture of what you aspire to achieve in the future. It's the North Star that guides your business's growth and development. A compelling vision paints a picture of success, inspiring you and your team to work toward a common goal.

Setting Clear Goals and Objectives

With your purpose and vision in mind, it's time to translate these lofty ideals into practical, actionable goals and objectives. Goals are the broader, overarching aims that align with your vision, while objectives are specific, measurable steps you take to achieve those goals.

Setting clear and SMART (Specific, Measurable, Achievable, Relevant, Time-bound) goals is essential. For example, if your purpose is to provide affordable and healthy food options in your community, a goal might be to open three new locations within the next three years. Objectives related to this goal could include securing funding, scouting suitable locations, and hiring staff.

Goal setting provides focus and direction, helping you prioritize tasks and allocate resources effectively. It also enables you to track your progress and make necessary adjustments along the way.

Crafting Your Unique Value Proposition

In today's competitive business landscape, differentiation is key. Your unique value proposition (UVP) defines what sets your business apart from the competition and why customers should choose you. It's a succinct statement that communicates the benefits of your product or service and the value it delivers to customers.

To craft an effective UVP, consider the following questions:

- What problem does your product or service solve?

- What unique features or qualities make your offering stand out?

- How does your business enhance the lives or experiences of your customers?

Your UVP should resonate with your target audience and address their pain points. It should be concise, memorable, and consistently communicated through your branding and marketing efforts.

Building a Solid Business Plan

A business plan is the roadmap that guides your business from its inception to its long-term goals. It's a comprehensive document that outlines your business's strategy, operations, and financial projections. A well-structured business plan serves several crucial purposes:

1. **Clarity:** It forces you to articulate your business concept, goals, and strategies clearly.

2. **Decision-Making:** It provides a framework for making informed decisions and managing risks.

3. **Communication:** It serves as a tool for attracting investors, partners, and lenders who want to understand your business.

4. **Benchmarking:** It offers a baseline for tracking your business's performance and adjusting your strategies as needed.

In this chapter, we will explore the key components of a business plan, including market research, financial projections, marketing strategies, and operational plans. A well-crafted business plan not only provides a roadmap for your business's future but also instills confidence in yourself and those who support your entrepreneurial journey.

As you embark on this foundational journey toward small business success, remember that your purpose, vision, goals, and plan will evolve over time. Flexibility and adaptability are essential traits for any small business owner. With a strong foundation, you can confidently tackle the challenges and opportunities that lie ahead.

Chapter 2: Legal Structure and Financial Management

In the realm of small business management, understanding the legal and financial aspects of your enterprise is paramount. This chapter delves deep into the critical elements of legal structure and financial management, providing you with essential insights to navigate this complex terrain successfully.

Choosing the Right Legal Structure

Selecting the appropriate legal structure for your small business is one of the most crucial decisions you'll make. The legal structure you choose will impact your taxes, liability, and overall business operations. Common legal structures for small businesses include:

1. **Sole Proprietorship:** This is the simplest form, where you and your business are essentially one entity. You have complete control but also bear full personal liability for business debts.

2. **Partnership:** In a partnership, two or more individuals share ownership and management responsibilities. Partnerships can be general (equal partnership) or limited (one partner has limited involvement or liability).

3. **Limited Liability Company (LLC):** An LLC combines the liability protection of a corporation with the simplicity of a sole proprietorship or partnership. Owners are typically not personally liable for business debts.

4. **Corporation:** Corporations are separate legal entities, shielding owners from personal liability. They have more complex formalities but offer various tax benefits.

5. **S Corporation:** An S Corp is a specific type of corporation that passes profits and losses through to the owners' individual tax returns, avoiding double taxation.

6. **Nonprofit Corporation:** If your business's primary purpose is not to make a profit but to serve a charitable, educational, or other non-

profitable cause, a nonprofit corporation is appropriate.

Choosing the right legal structure depends on factors like your business's size, industry, ownership structure, and tax considerations. Consult with legal and financial professionals to make an informed decision.

Bookkeeping and Financial Record-keeping

Maintaining accurate and organized financial records is the cornerstone of good financial management for your small business. Proper record-keeping allows you to:

- Track income and expenses

- Monitor cash flow

- Prepare accurate financial statements

- Comply with tax requirements

- Identify financial trends and areas for improvement

Consider implementing accounting software to streamline your record-keeping process. Regularly reconcile bank statements, categorize transactions, and maintain organized records of invoices, receipts, and financial documents. This practice not only ensures compliance with tax laws but also equips you with the data needed for informed decision-making.

Budgeting and Cash Flow Management

Budgeting is a critical financial management tool for small businesses. It involves creating a detailed plan that outlines your projected income and expenses over a specific period. A well-constructed budget helps you:

- Set financial goals
- Allocate resources effectively
- Identify potential financial shortfalls
- Control spending
- Plan for growth and expansion

Budgets should be flexible and regularly reviewed to reflect changing business conditions. Cash flow management, a subset of budgeting, focuses on monitoring the flow of money in and out of your business. Effective cash flow management ensures you have enough liquidity to meet your financial obligations, such as paying bills and covering payroll.

Understanding Your Financial Statements

Financial statements are the pulse of your small business. They provide a snapshot of your financial health and performance. Key financial statements include:

1. **Income Statement (Profit and Loss Statement):** This statement summarizes your revenues, costs, and expenses, providing a net profit or loss figure. It helps you track profitability over time.

2. **Balance Sheet:** This statement shows your business's assets, liabilities, and equity at a specific point in time. It provides a snapshot of your financial position.

3. **Cash Flow Statement:** This statement tracks the flow of cash in and out of your business. It shows how changes in your balance sheet and income statement affect cash and cash equivalents.

Understanding these financial statements is essential for making informed decisions, securing financing, and communicating your business's financial health to stakeholders.

In this chapter, we have explored the fundamental aspects of legal structure and financial management for small businesses. These foundational principles serve as the bedrock of your business's success. By choosing the right legal structure, maintaining meticulous financial records, budgeting wisely, and interpreting financial statements, you'll be well-equipped to steer your business towards a prosperous future.

Chapter 3: Small Business Tax Essentials

Navigating the intricacies of taxation is a critical aspect of small business management. This chapter delves into the essentials of small business taxation, equipping you with knowledge to handle taxes effectively, optimize deductions, maintain compliance, and minimize your tax liability.

Tax Basics for Small Businesses

Understanding the fundamental principles of taxation is essential for any small business owner. Here are some key tax concepts:

1. **Business Structure and Taxation:** The legal structure you choose for your business affects how you're taxed. Sole proprietors report business income on their personal tax returns, while partnerships, LLCs, and corporations have distinct tax obligations.

2. **Income Tax:** Small businesses are generally subject to federal and state income taxes.

Income tax is typically based on the net profit of the business after deducting allowable expenses.

3. **Self-Employment Tax:** If you're self-employed or a sole proprietor, you're responsible for paying self-employment tax, which covers Social Security and Medicare contributions.

4. **Sales Tax:** If your business sells physical products or certain services, you may be required to collect and remit sales tax to your state's tax authority.

5. **Employment Taxes:** If you have employees, you must withhold federal and state income taxes, Social Security, and Medicare taxes from their wages. You're also responsible for employer payroll taxes.

6. **Estimated Taxes:** Business owners typically make quarterly estimated tax payments to cover income and self-employment taxes. Accurate estimation helps prevent underpayment penalties.

Tax Deductions and Credits

Optimizing tax deductions and credits is a smart way to reduce your tax liability. Here are some deductions and credits commonly available to small businesses:

1. **Business Expenses:** Deductible business expenses include rent, utilities, office supplies, travel, and marketing costs. Keep meticulous records to substantiate these deductions.

2. **Home Office Deduction:** If you use part of your home exclusively for your business, you may be eligible for a home office deduction.

3. **Startup Expenses:** You can deduct certain costs associated with starting your business, such as legal fees and marketing expenses, up to a certain limit.

4. **Health Insurance Deduction:** Small business owners who pay for their health insurance premiums may qualify for a deduction.

5. **Small Business Tax Credits:** Depending on your circumstances, you may be eligible for tax credits like the Small Business Health Care Tax

Credit or the Research and Development (R&D) Tax Credit.

6. **Section 179 Deduction:** This allows businesses to deduct the cost of qualifying equipment and property purchases rather than depreciating them over time.

7. **Employee Benefits:** Providing benefits like retirement plans or education assistance can offer tax advantages for your business.

Understanding the eligibility criteria, documentation requirements, and limitations of these deductions and credits is essential to maximize your tax savings.

Compliance and Record-keeping

Small businesses must adhere to tax laws and regulations to avoid penalties and audits. Compliance involves:

1. **Filing Taxes:** File your federal and state tax returns accurately and on time, adhering to your chosen legal structure's tax requirements.

2. **Record-keeping:** Maintain organized financial records, receipts, invoices, and documentation

of all business transactions. Keep records for at least the recommended retention period (usually several years).

3. **Sales Tax Compliance:** If you collect sales tax, ensure timely remittance to the appropriate tax authority.

4. **Payroll Taxes:** Comply with payroll tax obligations, including timely withholding and remittance of employee taxes.

Strategies for Minimizing Tax Liability

Minimizing your tax liability involves strategic planning and proactive measures. Here are some strategies:

1. **Tax Planning:** Engage in year-round tax planning to optimize deductions, credits, and financial decisions.

2. **Hire a Tax Professional:** Consider working with a qualified tax advisor or accountant to ensure compliance and identify tax-saving opportunities.

3. **Retirement Planning:** Explore retirement plans like a Simplified Employee Pension (SEP) IRA or a 401(k) plan to reduce taxable income.

4. **Depreciation:** Utilize depreciation schedules to spread the cost of business assets over several years, reducing taxable income.

5. **Tax-efficient Business Structure:** Regularly assess whether your business structure remains the most tax-efficient choice as your business evolves.

6. **Charitable Contributions:** Make tax-deductible charitable contributions as a business, if applicable.

7. **Tax Credits:** Be aware of tax credits specific to your industry or location, such as energy-efficient equipment incentives or state-level incentives for job creation.

Mastering the essentials of small business taxation empowers you to navigate the tax landscape with confidence. By leveraging deductions, credits, compliance best practices, and strategic tax planning, you can optimize your tax situation and allocate more resources toward growing your business. Always consult with a tax professional for personalized guidance tailored to your unique business circumstances.

Chapter 4: The Art of Small Business Tax Planning

Tax planning is a dynamic and essential aspect of managing a small business effectively. In this chapter, we will explore the intricacies of tax planning, from year-round strategies to tax-efficient compensation, retirement, and estate planning, as well as staying informed about tax changes and regulations.

Year-round Tax Planning

Effective tax planning is not a once-a-year event; it's a year-round process. By proactively managing your tax situation throughout the year, you can optimize your financial position and minimize surprises come tax season. Here are key elements of year-round tax planning:

1. **Continuous Record-keeping:** Maintain meticulous financial records and keep your business transactions well-documented. This facilitates accurate tax reporting and deductions.

2. **Quarterly Estimated Taxes:** Make quarterly estimated tax payments to cover your income and self-employment taxes. This helps you avoid penalties for underpayment.

3. **Monitoring Tax Law Changes:** Stay informed about changes in tax laws and regulations, as they can significantly impact your business's tax liability. Consult with tax professionals to understand how these changes affect you.

4. **Expense Tracking:** Regularly review your expenses to identify tax-deductible items. Proper categorization can lead to significant tax savings.

5. **Asset Purchases:** Consider the timing of significant asset purchases and whether you can take advantage of deductions or depreciation.

6. **Profit and Loss Analysis:** Regularly analyze your profit and loss statement to identify areas where you can optimize revenue and reduce expenses.

Tax-efficient Compensation Strategies

Compensation strategies can have a significant impact on your tax liability as a small business owner. Here are some tax-efficient compensation strategies to consider:

1. **Salary vs. Dividends:** If you're the owner of a corporation, determine the most tax-efficient mix of salary and dividends for your income.

2. **Retirement Contributions:** Maximize contributions to retirement accounts like a SEP IRA or 401(k), which can reduce your taxable income while securing your financial future.

3. **Employee Benefits:** Provide tax-advantaged employee benefits like health insurance, retirement plans, or educational assistance to attract and retain talent.

4. **Hiring Family Members:** Employing family members can provide tax benefits, especially if they perform legitimate work for the business.

5. **Bonuses and Incentives:** Consider using bonuses and incentives strategically to motivate employees and reduce taxable income.

6. **Stock Options:** Explore equity-based compensation options that may offer tax advantages.

Retirement and Estate Planning

Retirement and estate planning are not just about securing your financial future; they also have tax implications. Here's how to integrate tax-efficient strategies into these areas:

1. **Retirement Plans:** Contribute as much as possible to retirement accounts. These contributions are often tax-deductible and can grow tax-free until retirement.

2. **Succession Planning:** Plan for the tax-efficient transfer of your business to family members or successors. Utilize strategies like gifting or trusts to minimize estate taxes.

3. **Tax-efficient Withdrawals:** When you begin taking distributions from retirement accounts,

consider the tax implications of your withdrawal strategy.

4. **Tax-efficient Investments:** Invest with an eye toward minimizing capital gains taxes and optimizing investment returns.

Navigating Tax Changes and Regulations

Tax laws and regulations can change frequently, impacting your business's tax situation. Here's how to navigate these changes effectively:

1. **Stay Informed:** Keep up-to-date with changes in tax laws at the federal, state, and local levels. Consult with tax professionals to understand the specific implications for your business.

2. **Plan Ahead:** Anticipate how changes in tax laws may affect your business and develop contingency plans if necessary.

3. **Consult Tax Professionals:** Work closely with tax advisors or accountants who specialize in small business taxation. They can provide guidance and ensure you're fully compliant.

4. **Lobby and Advocate:** If tax changes significantly impact your industry or business, consider participating in industry associations or advocacy groups that can influence tax policy.

Tax planning is both an art and a science. It requires diligence, adaptability, and a keen understanding of your business's financial dynamics. By implementing year-round strategies, optimizing compensation, planning for retirement and estate taxes, and staying informed about tax changes and regulations, you can master the art of small business tax planning and maximize your financial well-being.

Chapter 5: Growth Strategies for Small Businesses

In the ever-evolving world of entrepreneurship, recognizing the right time to scale your small business and implementing effective growth strategies are critical for long-term success. This chapter dives into the nuances of scaling, financing growth, marketing, branding, and building a high-performing team.

Recognizing When It's Time to Scale

Recognizing the opportune moment to scale your small business is often a delicate balance. Here are some signs that it might be time to expand:

1. **Consistent Demand:** If your product or service is in high demand and you struggle to meet it, expansion may be necessary to capture a larger market share.

2. **Profitable Operations:** If your business consistently generates healthy profits, you may have the financial stability to support growth.

3. **Saturated Market:** If your current market is saturated, expanding into new markets may provide opportunities for growth.

4. **Effective Systems:** Streamlined operations and efficient processes can indicate that your business is ready for expansion.

5. **Recurring Revenue Streams:** Reliable sources of recurring revenue, such as subscription models, can provide a stable foundation for growth.

6. **Competitive Advantages:** If you have unique offerings or a competitive edge, expanding can help capitalize on your strengths.

Financing Growth: Bootstrapping, Loans, and Investments

Scaling your business often requires financial resources. Here are various strategies for financing growth:

1. **Bootstrapping:** Many successful businesses start with minimal capital and grow organically through reinvested profits. This approach allows you to maintain control and equity.

2. **Loans:** Consider traditional loans, lines of credit, or Small Business Administration (SBA) loans to finance expansion. Ensure your business can handle the debt burden.

3. **Investment:** Seek investors or venture capital if you're comfortable sharing ownership and want access to additional resources, expertise, and networks.

4. **Crowdfunding:** Crowdfunding platforms allow you to raise funds from a wide audience, often in exchange for equity or rewards.

5. **Grants and Competitions:** Explore grants, competitions, and business incubators that offer financial support and resources to promising startups.

The right financing strategy depends on your business's growth stage, goals, and risk tolerance.

Marketing and Branding Strategies for Expansion

Expanding your small business requires strategic marketing and branding efforts. Here are key considerations:

1. **Market Research:** Conduct thorough market research to understand your target audience, competitors, and market trends. This knowledge informs your growth strategy.

2. **Digital Presence:** Enhance your online presence through a user-friendly website, search engine optimization (SEO), social media marketing, and content creation.

3. **Marketing Mix:** Develop a comprehensive marketing mix that may include digital advertising, email marketing, content marketing, and traditional advertising.

4. **Branding:** Strengthen your brand identity to communicate a consistent message that resonates with your audience.

5. **Customer Experience:** Deliver exceptional customer experiences to retain existing customers and attract new ones through word-of-mouth referrals.

6. **Local and Global Expansion:** Consider whether expansion should be local, regional, national, or

international based on your product/service and target market.

Hiring and Building a High-Performing Team

Scaling your business often requires expanding your team. Here's how to attract and nurture a high-performing workforce:

1. **Strategic Hiring:** Identify key roles and skills needed to support growth. Hire individuals who align with your company culture and values.

2. **Employee Development:** Invest in training and development programs to upskill your existing team and prepare them for new responsibilities.

3. **Leadership:** Build strong leadership within your organization to guide the team through growth.

4. **Culture and Morale:** Maintain a positive and inclusive company culture that encourages employee engagement and satisfaction.

5. **Performance Metrics:** Implement performance metrics and key performance indicators (KPIs) to measure employee performance and align it with business goals.

6. **Retention:** Employee retention is vital during expansion. Offer competitive compensation, benefits, and growth opportunities to retain top talent.

Remember that successful growth strategies involve constant adaptation and learning. It's essential to monitor progress, gather feedback, and adjust your approach as needed to ensure sustainable expansion.

In conclusion, growth is an exciting but challenging phase for small businesses. By recognizing the right time to scale, carefully considering financing options, implementing effective marketing and branding strategies, and building a high-performing team, you can navigate the path to expansion with confidence and increase your chances of long-term success.

Chapter 6: Leveraging Technology for Scalability

In the digital age, the strategic use of technology is often the linchpin for small business scalability. This chapter explores the integral role of technology in modern small businesses, automation and efficiency tools, data analytics for informed decision-making, and the crucial aspects of cybersecurity and data protection.

The Role of Technology in Modern Small Business

Technology has become the great equalizer for small businesses, enabling them to compete with larger counterparts and reach global markets. Here's how technology plays a pivotal role:

1. **Efficiency:** Technology streamlines operations, automates repetitive tasks, and reduces human errors, leading to greater efficiency.

2. **Market Reach:** Online platforms, e-commerce, and digital marketing extend the reach of small businesses far beyond their local markets.

3. **Data Insights:** Technology provides valuable data insights that inform business decisions and customer strategies.

4. **Customer Engagement:** Digital tools facilitate customer engagement through social media, email marketing, chatbots, and personalized experiences.

5. **Innovation:** Technology fosters innovation by allowing small businesses to develop new products, services, and business models.

6. **Scalability:** Technology scalability ensures that systems can grow with the business, accommodating increased data and user loads.

Automation and Efficiency Tools

Automation is a cornerstone of modern small business success. Here are ways to leverage automation for scalability:

1. **Workflow Automation:** Use tools like workflow management software to automate routine processes such as order processing, invoicing, and inventory management.

2. **Customer Relationship Management (CRM):** Implement a CRM system to automate lead tracking, customer communication, and sales processes.

3. **Email Marketing Automation:** Tools like Mailchimp and HubSpot automate email campaigns, segment audiences, and track customer engagement.

4. **Chatbots:** Deploy chatbots on your website or messaging platforms to handle customer inquiries and provide real-time assistance.

5. **Accounting Software:** Use accounting software like QuickBooks or Xero to automate financial processes, invoicing, and expense tracking.

6. **Inventory Management:** Implement inventory management software to optimize stock levels and automate reordering.

Data Analytics for Informed Decision-making

Data analytics empowers small businesses to make data-driven decisions, identify trends, and uncover opportunities for growth:

1. **Data Collection:** Use data collection tools to gather information from various sources, including customer behavior, website analytics, and sales data.

2. **Data Visualization:** Tools like Tableau and Power BI help visualize data, making it easier to identify patterns and insights.

3. **Predictive Analytics:** Predictive analytics models can forecast customer trends, inventory needs, and sales projections.

4. **Competitive Analysis:** Analyze competitor data to identify gaps in the market and areas where your business can differentiate.

5. **Customer Insights:** Use customer analytics to understand preferences, pain points, and buying behaviors.

6. **Marketing Optimization:** Data analytics can optimize marketing campaigns by identifying which strategies yield the best ROI.

Cybersecurity and Data Protection

With greater reliance on technology comes an increased need for cybersecurity and data protection measures:

1. **Data Encryption:** Encrypt sensitive data, both in transit and at rest, to protect it from unauthorized access.

2. **Firewalls and Antivirus Software:** Install robust firewalls and antivirus software to guard against malware and cyberattacks.

3. **Employee Training:** Train employees to recognize phishing attempts and practice safe cybersecurity habits.

4. **Regular Updates:** Keep software and systems up to date to patch security vulnerabilities.

5. **Data Backup:** Regularly back up critical data to prevent data loss in the event of a breach.

6. **Privacy Compliance:** Understand and adhere to data protection regulations, such as GDPR or HIPAA, depending on your industry and region.

7. **Incident Response Plan:** Develop a comprehensive incident response plan to address potential data breaches.

In summary, technology is the driving force behind modern small business scalability. By embracing automation, leveraging data analytics, and prioritizing cybersecurity and data protection, small businesses can harness the full potential of technology to grow, compete, and thrive in today's dynamic business landscape.

Chapter 7: Expanding Your Reach: Online and Offline

Expanding your business's reach, both online and offline, is crucial for growth and sustainability. This chapter explores how to create an effective online presence, employ e-commerce and digital marketing strategies, expand into new markets, and build strong customer relationships.

Creating an Effective Online Presence

In the digital era, establishing a compelling online presence is non-negotiable for small businesses. Here's how to do it effectively:

1. **Website:** Design a user-friendly website that reflects your brand, offers a seamless user experience, and provides valuable content.

2. **Social Media:** Maintain active profiles on platforms relevant to your target audience. Share engaging content and engage with your followers.

3. **Search Engine Optimization (SEO):** Optimize your website for search engines to increase its visibility in search results.

4. **Content Marketing:** Produce high-quality, relevant content such as blog posts, videos, and infographics that demonstrate your expertise and attract your target audience.

5. **Email Marketing:** Build an email list and send valuable content, promotions, and updates to your subscribers.

6. **Online Reviews:** Encourage satisfied customers to leave positive reviews on platforms like Google My Business, Yelp, and social media.

E-commerce and Digital Marketing Strategies

E-commerce and digital marketing are powerful tools for reaching a wider audience and driving sales:

1. **E-commerce Platform:** Choose a suitable e-commerce platform that aligns with your business needs, whether it's Shopify, WooCommerce, or a custom solution.

2. **Online Advertising:** Invest in online advertising through platforms like Google Ads, Facebook Ads, and Instagram to target specific demographics and interests.

3. **Social Commerce:** Leverage social media shopping features to make it easier for customers to purchase directly from your social profiles.

4. **Content Marketing:** Create content that educates, entertains, or solves problems for your target audience, positioning your brand as a trusted resource.

5. **Email Campaigns:** Use email marketing to nurture leads, recover abandoned carts, and promote new products or services.

6. **Remarketing:** Implement remarketing campaigns to re-engage website visitors who didn't make a purchase initially.

Expanding into New Markets

To expand your reach, consider moving beyond your current market:

1. **Market Research:** Conduct thorough research to identify new markets, both geographically and demographically, that align with your products or services.

2. **Local Expansion:** If feasible, open new physical locations or partner with local businesses to extend your presence.

3. **Global Expansion:** Explore international markets by assessing cultural, legal, logistical, and market-specific considerations.

4. **E-commerce Cross-border Selling:** Utilize e-commerce to sell products globally, leveraging platforms that facilitate international sales.

5. **Market Entry Strategies:** Choose the right market entry strategy, whether it's exporting, franchising, licensing, or forming strategic partnerships.

Building Strong Customer Relationships

Strong customer relationships are the bedrock of business success. Here's how to nurture them:

1. **Personalization:** Tailor your interactions to individual customer preferences and needs.

2. **Customer Support:** Provide exceptional customer support through multiple channels, including chat, email, phone, and social media.

3. **Loyalty Programs:** Reward loyal customers with incentives like discounts, exclusive access, or loyalty points.

4. **Feedback and Surveys:** Actively seek feedback from customers and use it to improve your products, services, and overall experience.

5. **Community Building:** Create a community around your brand by encouraging customer interactions, hosting events, and fostering a sense of belonging.

6. **Transparency:** Be transparent about your products, pricing, and policies to build trust with your customers.

Expanding your business reach, both online and offline, requires a multifaceted approach that integrates technology, marketing strategies, market research, and customer relationship building. By following these guidelines, you can not only broaden your business's horizons but also strengthen its foundations for sustained growth and success.

Chapter 8: Scaling Sustainably

Scaling your business is an exciting endeavor, but it comes with its own set of challenges. This chapter delves into the importance of scaling sustainably and offers insights into managing risks, maintaining quality and customer satisfaction, adapting to market changes, and forming strategic partnerships and alliances.

Managing Risks During Growth

1. **Financial Risk:** As your business expands, financial risks increase. It's crucial to maintain strong financial management, monitor cash flow, and have contingency plans for unexpected expenses.

2. **Operational Risk:** Rapid growth can strain your operations. Continually assess and optimize your processes to ensure they can handle increased demand efficiently.

3. **Market Risk:** Expanding into new markets or introducing new products/services exposes you

to market fluctuations. Diversify your offerings and customer base to mitigate this risk.

4. **Compliance and Regulatory Risk:** As your business grows, compliance requirements may change. Stay informed about industry regulations and adjust your practices accordingly.

5. **Talent Risk:** Attracting and retaining skilled employees becomes essential during expansion. Develop talent management strategies, offer competitive compensation, and invest in training and development.

Maintaining Quality and Customer Satisfaction

1. **Quality Control:** As you scale, maintaining product or service quality is paramount. Implement quality control measures, conduct regular checks, and seek customer feedback for improvement.

2. **Customer Service:** Exceptional customer service remains a top priority. Ensure your customer support team can handle increased inquiries promptly and efficiently.

3. **Communication:** Keep customers informed about changes, improvements, and new offerings to maintain transparency and trust.

4. **Feedback Loops:** Create feedback loops to capture customer insights and use them to refine your products, services, and overall customer experience.

5. **Scalable Systems:** Invest in scalable systems and technologies that can grow with your business while maintaining quality standards.

Adapting to Market Changes

1. **Market Research:** Continuously monitor market trends and customer preferences to adapt your business strategies accordingly.

2. **Agility:** Foster a culture of adaptability and innovation within your organization. Encourage employees to propose and implement changes when necessary.

3. **Product/Service Evolution:** Be prepared to evolve your offerings based on market feedback and changing customer needs.

4. **Competitive Analysis:** Stay vigilant about your competitors' actions and adapt your strategies to maintain your competitive edge.

5. **Customer-Centric Approach:** Focus on delivering what your customers want rather than being rigid in your offerings.

Strategic Partnerships and Alliances

1. **Identifying Opportunities:** Look for potential partners or alliances that complement your business goals and fill gaps in your capabilities.

2. **Due Diligence:** Conduct thorough due diligence when considering partnerships or alliances to ensure alignment in values, goals, and objectives.

3. **Mutual Benefits:** Develop partnerships that offer mutual benefits, such as shared resources, access to new markets, or cost savings.

4. **Clear Agreements:** Draft clear, legally binding agreements that outline the roles, responsibilities, and expectations of each party.

5. **Relationship Building:** Nurture your partnerships and alliances by fostering open communication and maintaining a positive working relationship.

Scaling sustainably is about balancing growth with stability, and it requires careful planning, risk management, and a commitment to maintaining quality and customer satisfaction. By staying adaptable, informed about market changes, and open to strategic partnerships, your business can navigate the challenges of growth while ensuring its long-term success.

Chapter 9: The Human Element: Leadership and Team Development

In the realm of small business management, the human element is often the most critical factor in success. This chapter explores the significance of leadership, the development of leadership skills, building a strong company culture, and the importance of employee training and development.

The Role of Leadership in Small Business Success

Effective leadership is the cornerstone of small business success. Leaders set the vision, provide direction, and inspire their teams to achieve goals. Here's how leadership contributes to success:

1. **Vision and Strategy:** Leaders define a clear vision for the business and develop strategies to achieve it.

2. **Decision-Making:** Leaders make crucial decisions that impact the business, such as

resource allocation, product development, and market expansion.

3. **Motivation:** Effective leaders inspire and motivate employees, fostering a culture of dedication and commitment.

4. **Problem Solving:** Leaders are adept at identifying and solving problems, whether they're operational, financial, or strategic.

5. **Adaptability:** In an ever-changing business landscape, leaders must adapt to new challenges and opportunities.

6. **Team Building:** Leaders assemble and lead high-performing teams, ensuring that each member contributes to the company's success.

Developing Leadership Skills

Leadership skills can be developed and refined over time. Here's how to nurture your leadership abilities:

1. **Self-awareness:** Understand your strengths and weaknesses as a leader and continually work on self-improvement.

2. **Communication:** Effective leaders are skilled communicators who can convey their vision and expectations clearly.

3. **Decision-Making:** Practice making informed, timely decisions, and learn from both successes and failures.

4. **Empathy:** Develop empathy to understand and connect with your team members on a personal level.

5. **Adaptability:** Embrace change and adapt to new circumstances with resilience and flexibility.

6. **Strategic Thinking:** Cultivate a strategic mindset by analyzing situations and considering long-term implications.

7. **Conflict Resolution:** Hone your conflict resolution skills to maintain a harmonious work environment.

Building a Strong Company Culture

Company culture is the collective values, beliefs, and behaviors that define your organization. It's shaped by leadership and impacts every aspect of your business. Here's how to build a strong company culture:

1. **Lead by Example:** Demonstrate the values and behaviors you want to see in your employees.

2. **Clarify Values:** Clearly define your company's core values and communicate them to all team members.

3. **Employee Involvement:** Involve employees in shaping the culture by seeking their input and feedback.

4. **Recognition and Rewards:** Acknowledge and reward employees who embody the desired culture.

5. **Continuous Improvement:** Regularly assess and refine your company culture to ensure it aligns with your business goals.

Employee Training and Development

Investing in employee training and development is a key strategy for business growth. Here's how to approach it:

1. **Assessment:** Identify skill gaps and training needs within your organization.

2. **Structured Training Programs:** Develop structured training programs that cover essential skills and knowledge.

3. **On-the-Job Learning:** Encourage learning through on-the-job experiences, mentorship, and coaching.

4. **Professional Development:** Support employees' professional growth by providing opportunities for additional education and certifications.

5. **Feedback and Evaluation:** Continually assess the effectiveness of your training programs and adjust them as needed.

6. **Career Pathing:** Help employees define clear career paths within your organization.

7. **Recognition:** Recognize and reward employees who actively participate in training and contribute to their personal and professional growth.

Leadership and team development are ongoing processes that require commitment and investment. By cultivating effective leadership, nurturing a strong company culture, and prioritizing employee training and development, small businesses can create a thriving and motivated workforce that contributes to long-term success.

Chapter 10: Measuring Success and Continual Improvement

In the world of small business management, measuring success and continually improving operations are essential for sustained growth and competitiveness. This chapter explores the significance of key performance indicators (KPIs), performance metrics and benchmarks, adapting to feedback and market trends, and fostering a continuous improvement mindset.

Key Performance Indicators (KPIs) for Small Businesses

KPIs are critical metrics that quantify the performance and progress of your business. When chosen thoughtfully, KPIs provide valuable insights into your business's health. Here's how to select and use KPIs effectively:

1. **Relevance:** Identify KPIs that align with your business goals and objectives. Consider financial, operational, customer-related, and growth-focused KPIs.

2. **Specificity:** Make sure KPIs are specific and measurable, enabling you to track progress over time.

3. **Data Accessibility:** Ensure you have access to the data needed to measure your chosen KPIs accurately.

4. **Real-time Monitoring:** Whenever possible, choose KPIs that can be monitored in real time to enable proactive decision-making.

5. **Benchmarking:** Compare your KPIs to industry benchmarks to gauge your performance relative to competitors.

Common KPIs for small businesses include revenue growth, customer acquisition cost, customer lifetime value, gross profit margin, inventory turnover, website traffic, conversion rates, and employee productivity.

Performance Metrics and Benchmarks

In addition to KPIs, performance metrics and benchmarks help you assess and improve your business's operations:

1. **Operational Metrics:** These metrics delve into the efficiency of your day-to-day operations, such as production cycle time, order fulfillment accuracy, and inventory levels.

2. **Customer Satisfaction Metrics:** Measure customer satisfaction through surveys, feedback, and Net Promoter Score (NPS) to identify areas for improvement.

3. **Financial Metrics:** Monitor financial health by tracking metrics like cash flow, profitability ratios, and return on investment (ROI).

4. **Employee Productivity Metrics:** Assess workforce efficiency through metrics like employee turnover, productivity per employee, and training hours.

5. **Market Benchmarks:** Compare your business's performance to industry benchmarks, such as revenue growth rates, market share, and customer retention rates.

Benchmarking helps you identify areas where you're excelling or falling short compared to peers or industry standards. It can provide insights into areas that require improvement.

Adapting to Feedback and Market Trends

Feedback from customers, employees, and market trends offers invaluable insights that drive improvement:

1. **Customer Feedback:** Actively seek and listen to customer feedback to identify pain points and areas for enhancement in your products or services.

2. **Employee Feedback:** Encourage employees to provide feedback on internal processes, systems, and company culture.

3. **Market Trends:** Stay informed about industry trends, emerging technologies, and shifts in consumer behavior to adapt your strategies accordingly.

4. **Competitor Analysis:** Regularly assess your competitors' actions and strategies to identify opportunities for differentiation.

5. **Data Analysis:** Analyze data from various sources to detect patterns and trends that can inform strategic decisions.

The Continuous Improvement Mindset

A continuous improvement mindset is the foundation for ongoing success. Here's how to foster it within your organization:

1. **Cultivate a Learning Culture:** Encourage a culture of learning, where employees are motivated to seek knowledge and improve their skills.

2. **Feedback Loops:** Implement feedback loops to capture insights from customers, employees, and stakeholders.

3. **Root Cause Analysis:** When issues arise, dig deep to identify the root causes rather than addressing surface-level symptoms.

4. **Experimentation:** Be open to experimentation and innovation, even if it means occasional failures.

5. **Process Optimization:** Continuously refine and optimize your business processes to eliminate inefficiencies.

6. **Agility:** Be prepared to adapt to changing circumstances swiftly.

7. **Goal Setting:** Set clear, achievable goals for improvement and track progress toward those goals.

The continuous improvement mindset ensures that your small business remains agile, responsive to customer needs, and capable of thriving in a dynamic business environment.

Measuring success, setting benchmarks, adapting to feedback, and fostering a culture of continuous improvement are integral to the long-term success of your small business. By focusing on these principles, you can continually enhance your operations, drive growth, and remain competitive in your industry.

Conclusion

The Small Business Journey: Reflection and Future Planning

As we conclude this comprehensive guide to small business management, it's essential to take a moment for reflection and future planning. Your journey as a small business owner is a remarkable one filled with challenges, triumphs, and continuous growth. Let's recap the key takeaways and explore the path forward.

The Ever-evolving Landscape of Small Business Management

Small businesses are the lifeblood of economies worldwide, and their importance cannot be overstated. In an ever-evolving business landscape, staying relevant and thriving as a small business requires a blend of adaptability, innovation, and resilience. Here are some key points to reflect upon:

1. **Diverse Challenges:** Small business management presents diverse challenges, from financial hurdles and market competition to the

changing dynamics of customer behavior and technological advancements.

2. **Importance of Leadership:** Effective leadership is at the core of small business success. As a leader, your vision, decision-making, and ability to inspire and guide your team are pivotal.

3. **Strategic Thinking:** Strategic thinking is your compass in navigating the complexities of business. It involves setting clear objectives, identifying opportunities, and making informed decisions.

4. **Financial Management:** Sound financial management is crucial. Maintaining a healthy cash flow, understanding your financial statements, and optimizing tax planning are essential components.

5. **Technology Integration:** Leveraging technology for efficiency, marketing, data analytics, and cybersecurity is a fundamental aspect of modern small business management.

6. **Customer-Centric Approach:** A customer-centric approach is vital for building strong

relationships, fostering loyalty, and staying ahead of market trends.

7. **Continuous Improvement:** Embrace a continuous improvement mindset. Regularly assess your performance, adapt to feedback, and refine your strategies to remain competitive.

Your Roadmap to Long-term Success

As you move forward in your small business journey, here's your roadmap to long-term success:

1. **Define Your Vision:** Revisit and refine your business's purpose and vision. Know what you stand for and where you want to go.

2. **Set Clear Goals:** Establish clear, achievable goals and objectives. Ensure they are specific, measurable, and aligned with your vision.

3. **Embrace Innovation:** Stay open to innovation and change. Keep an eye on emerging technologies, market trends, and customer preferences.

4. **Cultivate Leadership:** Invest in developing your leadership skills and fostering a leadership culture within your organization.

5. **Prioritize Customer Relationships:** Continuously seek to understand and serve your customers better. Their satisfaction and loyalty are the keys to your success.

6. **Strategic Planning:** Regularly review and adjust your business strategies. Ensure they remain aligned with your goals and the evolving business landscape.

7. **Invest in Your Team:** Nurture your employees' growth and development. A motivated and skilled team is your greatest asset.

8. **Monitor and Adapt:** Keep a close watch on performance metrics, benchmarks, and KPIs. Use this data to adapt, make informed decisions, and improve continuously.

9. **Foster a Learning Culture:** Encourage a culture of learning, curiosity, and innovation within your organization. Challenge the status quo and seek opportunities for improvement.

10.   **Plan for the Future:** Anticipate future challenges and opportunities. Develop contingency plans and strategies that position your business for long-term sustainability.

In the dynamic world of small business management, adaptability is key. Embrace change, learn from your experiences, and continue to evolve. Remember that your journey is unique, and while this guide provides a solid foundation, your individual experiences will shape your path to success.

As you navigate the ever-evolving landscape of small business management, keep your vision in focus, your strategies adaptable, and your commitment to excellence unwavering. Your small business has the potential to not only thrive but also leave a lasting impact on your community and the broader world of commerce. Embrace the journey with enthusiasm, and may your future be filled with success, growth, and fulfillment.

Appendices

Resources for Small Business Owners

As a small business owner, access to valuable resources can be a game-changer. Here's a curated list of resources to help you on your journey:

1. **Small Business Administration (SBA):** The SBA offers a wealth of resources, including guides, training, and access to financing options for small businesses. Visit their website at www.sba.gov.

2. **SCORE:** SCORE is a nonprofit organization that provides free mentoring, workshops, and resources to small business owners. Find a local SCORE chapter or access their online resources at www.score.org.

3. **U.S. Chamber of Commerce:** The U.S. Chamber of Commerce provides advocacy and resources for businesses of all sizes. Visit their website at www.uschamber.com.

4. **Small Business Development Centers (SBDCs):** SBDCs offer free consulting and low-cost

training services to help you start and grow your business. Find your local SBDC at www.americassbdc.org.

5. **National Federation of Independent Business (NFIB):** NFIB provides advocacy, resources, and research specifically tailored to small business owners. Explore their offerings at www.nfib.com.

6. **Small Business Resources by State:** Many states offer their own resources for small businesses. Check your state's official website or visit the SBA's state-specific resources page.

7. **Online Learning Platforms:** Platforms like Coursera, LinkedIn Learning, and Udemy offer a wide range of courses on business management, entrepreneurship, and specific skills.

8. **Business Forums:** Join online communities like Reddit's r/smallbusiness, StartupNation, and the Small Business Forum to connect with fellow entrepreneurs and seek advice.

9. **Books and Publications:** Explore books on entrepreneurship and small business management. Classic titles like "The Lean Startup" by Eric Ries and "Good to Great" by Jim Collins offer valuable insights.

Glossary of Small Business Management Terms

1. **Bootstrapping:** Funding a business with personal savings or revenue generated by the business itself, rather than seeking external financing.

2. **Cash Flow:** The movement of money in and out of a business, indicating its liquidity and ability to meet financial obligations.

3. **ROI (Return on Investment):** A measure of the profitability of an investment, expressed as a percentage of the initial investment.

4. **SWOT Analysis:** An assessment that identifies a business's Strengths, Weaknesses, Opportunities, and Threats to inform strategic planning.

5. **P&L Statement (Profit and Loss Statement):** A financial statement that summarizes a business's revenue, costs, and expenses to determine its profitability over a specific period.

6. **Market Research:** The process of gathering and analyzing data about a target market, including customer preferences, behavior, and market trends.

7. **Cash Flow Statement:** A financial statement that tracks the flow of cash in and out of a business, including operating, investing, and financing activities.

8. **Business Plan:** A comprehensive document outlining a business's goals, strategies, financial projections, and operational details.

9. **E-commerce:** The buying and selling of goods and services over the internet.

10. **SEO (Search Engine Optimization):** Strategies and techniques used to improve a website's visibility on search engines like Google.

Sample Business Plan Template

A well-structured business plan is crucial for small business success. You can find sample business plan templates and guides at the following sources:

1. **SBA Business Plan Template:** www.sba.gov

2. **SCORE Business Plan Templates:** www.score.org

These resources and appendices are valuable tools for small business owners to reference as they navigate the complexities of entrepreneurship. Whether you're seeking guidance, templates, or terminology explanations, these resources are designed to support your journey toward small business success.

"Small Business Mastery: Tax Planning and Scaling Strategies" is a comprehensive guide designed to empower small business owners and aspiring entrepreneurs with the knowledge and tools needed to navigate the intricate world of tax planning and strategic growth. From mastering the fundamentals of small business management to developing tax-efficient strategies and scaling your venture sustainably, this book serves as an invaluable resource for anyone looking to build and expand a successful small business. Whether you're just starting or have an established business, the insights within these pages will help you take your entrepreneurial journey to the next level.